ANIME AND MANGA CREATORS

The Early Years

Marc Hairston and Pamela Gossin

About the Authors

Marc Hairston was a young child with two loves: space and cartoons. Now as an old adult, he is a professional space physicist studying satellite data to see how the sun and the solar wind affect the earth's atmosphere and cause the northern lights. In his spare time he has become an anime scholar, giving talks and writing papers and books. He has stacks of unopened anime Blu-ray discs and calculates it will take over ten years to get through the backlog of unwatched shows.

—For my favorite anime fans: my son, Roberto, and my two "goddaughters," Sofia and Cathy.

Pamela Gossin is a professor of the history of science and literature who studies and writes about how the humanities and sciences can both teach us meaningful things about ourselves and the world around us. Together, she and Marc Hairston have taught many anime and manga classes, including Science Fiction and Fantasy, and Healing Nature. Like Princess Nausicaä, she tries to appreciate the beauty and complexity of the universe and live in harmony with nature and other living beings.

— For Victor and our newly arrived grand-twins, Greyson and Richard—so blessed to share the universe with you!

Printed in the United States

For more information, contact:
ReferencePoint Press, Inc.
PO Box 27779
San Diego, CA 92198
www.ReferencePointPress.com

Picture Credits:
Cover: Aflo Co. Ltd./Alamy Stock Photo
5: Associated Press
10: Manuel Esteban/Shutterstock
12: Kyodo/Newscom
17: Kyodo/Newscom
21: Wire.Dog/Alamy Stock Photo
25: TOKUMA SHOTEN/Album/Newscom
30: Moviestore Collection Ltd/Alamy Stock Photo
34: Associated Press
36: Collection Christophel/Alamy Stock Photo
40: Associated Press
43: Associated Press
46: Associated Press
50: Collection Christophel/Alamy Stock Photo
53: Patti McConville/Alamy Stock Photo
56: Photo 12/Alamy Stock Photo

LIBRARY OF CONGRESS CATALOGING-IN-PUBLICATION DATA

Names: Hairston, Marc author | Gossin, Pamela author
Title: Anime and manga creators : the early years / by Marc Hairston and Pamela Gossin.
Description: San Diego, CA : ReferencePoint Press, 2025. | Includes bibliographical references and index.
Identifiers: LCCN 2025009889 (print) | LCCN 2025009890 (ebook) | ISBN 9781678210946 library binding | ISBN 9781678210953 ebook
Subjects: LCSH: Manga (Comic books)--Juvenile literature | Anime (Motion pictures)--Juvenile literature | Cartoonists--Japan--Biography--Juvenile literature | LCGFT: Comics criticism | Film criticism | Biographies
Classification: LCC PN6790.J3 H25 2025 (print) | LCC PN6790.J3 (ebook) | DDC 741.5/952 [B]--dc23/eng/20250313
LC record available at https://lccn.loc.gov/2025009889
LC ebook record available at https://lccn.loc.gov/2025009890

CONTENTS

The Making of Classic Anime and Manga

In the early years, no one knew for sure whether anime and manga would be successful forms of entertainment and visual storytelling. Now there is evidence all around us that they have become massively popular, not only in Japan but around the world. Of course, exciting new releases continue to attract new viewers and readers, but what is surprising is that some anime and manga—created way back in the mid-twentieth century—are still just as popular as ever. These works are now considered classics.

Classic anime and manga are especially recognized and appreciated for their creative artistry, relatable characters, and intriguing and meaningful plotlines. Their lasting appeal spans decades and connects multiple generations, from children and teens to young adults, parents, and grandparents. Some classics were instant hits, while others grew devoted fan bases more slowly. Most were created by writers and animators whom everyone has heard of, but some were inspired by hidden gems and little-known geniuses who deserve to be known better. Both *shōnen* (boys) and *shōjo* (girls) stories have now attained classic status.

What Is Old Is New

Classic anime and manga have popped up everywhere across Japanese culture, proving that—as the saying goes—what is old is new. A perfect example of this was on full display at the

Expo 2025 world's fair in Osaka, Japan. Outside one of the pavilions, a truly giant (50 feet [15 m] tall) full-scale model of the RX-78 Gundam appeared with a new look. Instead of the traditional upright stance so often used in the original *Mobile Suit Gundam* forty-five years ago, in this exhibit, a Tokyo-based reporter writes, the Gundam is shown "kneeling down with a hand outstretched towards the heavens, a pose chosen to evoke feelings of reaching for the future and outer space."[1] Indeed, this model from another era looked as though it had just arrived and was ready to leap into new adventures.

Classic anime and manga never seem to get old. At the Expo 2025 world's fair in Japan, a giant model of the forty-five-year-old RX-78 Gundam is on display with a new stance and ready for new adventures.

In a similar leap across time, announcements of a new anime film version of Riyoko Ikeda's *The Rose of Versailles* appeared in January 2025. The original manga for this series debuted over fifty years ago. Since *Hello Kitty* was celebrating her fiftieth birthday at the same time, she shared the fun with the main characters from the *Rose* franchise. In classic *kawaii* (cute) style, Hello Kitty and three of her friends appeared in a cosplay cross-promotion with Kitty-chan herself dressed as Lady Oscar, My Melody as Queen Marie Antoinette, Dear Daniel as André Grandier, and Pocchaco as Hans Axel von Fersen.

Elements of classic anime and manga have also leaped from screens into real life. When a reboot of Rumiko Takahashi's *Ranma ½* anime series recently premiered worldwide on Netflix, it ranked number six of all non-English shows on that platform and attracted over 1.4 million viewers. At the same time, taking advantage of audiences hungry for the 1989 original, three *Ranma ½*–themed cafés opened in Japan, with their decor re-creating the visual vibe used in the show. The famous gender-bending story revolves around a curse whereby a splash of cold water causes the main character to change from a boy to a girl and hot water changes him back into a boy. So, in keeping with this theme, as writer Casey Baseel notes, the cafés offered "two different Ranma-themed dishes, each with a bit of temperature-based transformation involved."[2] One was served with a bucket of hot beef broth and the other a chilled bowl of tomato soup.

Then Is Now

From the day they first appeared, early manga and anime classics have continuously influenced the creation of new versions of themselves and inspired new fan favorites. Some of the earliest storylines, characters, and shows are still sparking new spin-offs, new kinds of merchandise and games, and new live-theater and media productions. One important reason why some stories become classics is because, like fairy tales and fables, they engage universal and timeless themes that almost every reader and viewer can relate to. Then and now, past and present human beings have a lot in common. Classic storytelling helps audiences navigate issues of loneliness and belonging, the confusion and challenges of growing up, illness, loss of friendships, and the end of life. Some classic anime and manga present stories that immerse readers and viewers in realistic depictions of natural beauty and uplifting moments of daily life. Others present imaginative fantasy visions of human potential and inspiring examples of heroic courage.

spin-off
Separate, new stories (in anime or manga form) that have been inspired by the originals but can be read or viewed as standalone works

Another reason why particular anime and manga become classics is because of the individual personalities and artistic gifts of the writers and animators who create them. Learning more about the unique lives and experiences of classic anime artists and manga writers can help us understand where great works of anime and manga come from and why they still matter.

CHAPTER ONE

Kenji Miyazawa and *Night on the Galactic Railroad*

Although Kenji Miyazawa was born and died before manga and anime became established as popular forms of storytelling and visual entertainment, his imaginative stories and poems have had a profound effect on the creation of both for nearly one hundred years. He is known for the visual imagery in his poetry and fiction and his insightful way of observing and describing the beauty and meaning of the natural world. Those qualities have directly influenced many manga and anime creators' use of visual symbols and depictions of plants, animals, and the environment in later works.

Born in 1896 in Hanamaki in the Japanese prefecture of Iwate, Miyazawa was the eldest son of a wealthy pawnbroker in a village of poor rice farmers. As a teenager he converted to a service-oriented type of Buddhism and devoted himself to making the conditions of life better for all living things on earth. His religious beliefs also led him to reject taking over his parents' profitable business, as it seemed morally wrong to him for his family to benefit from the misfortune and poverty of others. Instead, Miyazawa chose to attend college and train in agriculture and geology. After graduation, he returned to Hanamaki to teach high school. He also founded a cooperative to educate local farmers in new, scientific agricultural techniques.

Beliefs and Influences

Miyazawa lived by the philosophy that every human was of equal value and deserving of compassion and caring. He believed that all living beings and nonliving things are one, as everything is part of and deeply connected to the infinite energy and wonder of the universe. He tried his best to put his beliefs and ideas into real-world action through everything he did.

In the classroom and in his fieldwork, he employed unusual teaching methods. He often took his students on nature walks, during which he encouraged them to talk to and listen to the plants, animals, and even the stones. When he noticed something beautiful—such as unusual cloud formations, the complex structure of an ancient tree, or the patterns on a passing butterfly's wings—he would even stop in the middle of a lesson to write a poem. He also understood the importance of teaching by doing. He actively experimented with new planting techniques and natural fertilizers that might improve the soil and worked alongside farmers in the fields to test these methods and products. During times of famine, Miyazawa refused to consume the meals his well-to-do family prepared for him unless the farmers and their families also had enough to eat.

parables
Brief stories that offer a moral lesson or spiritual truth that can be used as a guide in human life

During his short life (he died from pneumonia at age thirty-seven), Miyazawa wrote hundreds of poems and children's stories, but he only published two books. Both appeared in 1924. In April of that year, he published a collected volume of his poetry entitled *Spring and the Demon*. In December, *The Restaurant of Many Orders* appeared in print. It offered a selection of his children's stories, parables, and fairy tales. Although neither of his books sold many copies, the visual imagery, meaningful symbols, and deep emotions he created in his verses and narratives attracted the attention of some notable poets and literary writers of the time. After his death, these admirers and his closest friends organized his remaining writings and published them.

Kenji Miyazawa (honored with a commemorative postage stamp) did not live to see manga and anime become popular forms of storytelling and visual entertainment. But his imaginative stories and poems have had a profound effect on both for nearly one hundred years.

In this literary afterlife, Miyazawa's poems, fairy tales, and stories began to reach a still-expanding audience. They now have been read and treasured by millions of readers of all ages, throughout Japan and the world.

Best-Known Work

Kenji Miyazawa's best-known work is *Night on the Galactic Railroad*. Written as a children's novella (short novel), the story describes a fantastic train ride through the night sky to the afterlife. The plot was inspired by real events. In 1922 Miyazawa's beloved younger sister, Toshi, died at age twenty-four. While deeply grieving her loss, Miyazawa traveled alone on a long night train. Riding for miles across the dark landscape all through the night, he wondered whether there was life after death and what might have happened to his sister's soul. Images from this train trip, blended with the complex thoughts and feelings that he experienced that night, formed the seeds of this special and tender story.

In *Night on the Galactic Railroad* two young schoolboys, Giovanni and Campanella, attend the late-summer nighttime Centaurus Festival, when villagers traditionally float candle-lit gourds down

novella

A work of prose fiction that is longer than a short story but shorter than a full-length novel and often offers an in-depth study of one character or an emotionally significant event

Anime That Draws on Miyazawa's Works and Life

Several lovely anime films have been based on Kenji Miyazawa's unusual life and short stories. *Gauche the Cellist* (1982), written and animated by Isao Takahata, adapts Miyazawa's story of a mediocre cellist who improves his musical performance after interacting with several woodland creatures. (At one point in his life, Miyazawa also learned to play the cello.) *The Life of Budori Gusuko* (2012) follows Miyazawa's story of a young man who (very much like Miyazawa himself) tries to be a farmer and learn science to improve the world. Animated by Gisaburo Sugii, the director of *Night on the Galactic Railroad*, all the characters are cast as cartoon cats. In *Spring and Chaos* (1996), animator Shoji Kawamori uses surreal imagery to portray Miyazawa's life, creativity, and unique vision. His use of psychedelic colors and sounds may represent scholars' speculations that Miyazawa had synesthesia—a neurological condition in which a person experiences sensory crossover ("seeing" shapes and colors while hearing music, or "tasting" sounds). And, as in other versions of Miyazawa's most famous story, the human characters are drawn as anthropomorphic cats.

the river after dark. Also referred to as the Festival of Stars in the story, this ceremony is likely based on Japan's real Toro Nagashi Lantern Festival that commemorates the souls of the dead. In early scenes, the boys interact with their teacher and classmates, family, and village merchants. Giovanni's father has been long absent from his family, traveling great distances to earn a living by fishing. Schoolmates tease Giovanni about his father's unkept promises and gossip that maybe his dad has not returned because he has done something illegal. Miyazawa describes Giovanni's inner thoughts as he tries to understand the senseless cruelty of their comments. In a series of poignant moments Giovanni fulfills multiple responsibilities as he tries to be a good student, a good person, and a good friend. He works part time after school to help support his family, and he cares for his long-ill mother, who is perhaps recovering but remains too weak to leave her bed.

On the evening of the festival, the two boys find themselves sharing a train ride, but instead of traveling on the ground, the

A steam locomotive on an illuminated bridge in Japan recreates the world imagined by Kenji Miyazawa in Night on the Galactic Railroad. *Miyazawa's famous story revolves around two young boys who make a remarkable celestial journey by train.*

locomotive flies up into the sky and beyond, making brief stops at important celestial stations along the Milky Way. The boys encounter various travelers who get on the train briefly and then depart at different stops. These travelers represent the souls of the dead, and all of them are journeying to different kinds of afterlives.

Hopeful and Uplifting

During this journey, the two friends discuss the meaning of life, the nature of happiness, and what it means to sacrifice oneself for others. At the end, Campanella also exits the train, leaving a distraught and crying Giovanni completely alone. Giovanni then returns to the village, where he discovers that Campanella had drowned when he jumped into the river to save a classmate. Giovanni realizes that their trip on the Galactic Railroad was to accompany his friend on his final journey to the afterlife.

Despite its serious themes of death and loss, the story ultimately feels hopeful and uplifting. First published in 1934, the year after Miyazawa's death, it became very popular throughout Japan. After World War II *Night on the Galactic Railroad* was read in Japanese elementary and middle schools. The goal was to gently introduce the idea of mortality and loss to young students in much the same way that *Charlotte's Web* has been used in US schools for the same purpose.

Through this story, generations of future Japanese animators and manga artists were also introduced to Miyazawa's beautiful vision of human life, the natural world, and the universe. Across many decades, anime and manga creators have developed adaptations of this story and have frequently used allusions to his imagery and poetry in their works.

Traveling to the Big Screen

Around the fiftieth anniversary of *Night on the Galactic Railroad*'s first publication, animation director Gisaburo Sugii and manga artist Hiroshi Masumura created an anime film version of the story. Released in 1984, the anime was based on Masumura's manga version of the novel—a version that included a strange but intriguing creative change. As the novella had become very well known over the years, Masumura feared that everyone in Japan had already formed their own mental images of the characters and that any character designs he came up with would disappoint his audience. To avoid this problem, he decided to draw the characters in the manga as anthropomorphic cats.

The anime followed the example Masumura had set. Nearly all of the characters were cast as cats. To this day, "Why cats?" remains one of the most frequently asked questions about this anime. As Masumura explained, if "you set down a human face to this story, it changes the feeling of the story entirely, defining it around your own image, and I wanted to avoid that. I wouldn't have bothered to give it this much thought if the story didn't mean as much to me as it does."[3] This artistic choice was also ironic because apparently in real life Miyazawa disliked cats.

Another unusual facet of the film is that it incorporated the artificial language of Esperanto into all the written texts and signs that appear in the backgrounds. Invented in the 1880s to be a universal second language, Esperanto was intended to help everyone around the world communicate across cultures and language differences. Given his utopian vision of global unity, Miyazawa embraced the idea of Esperanto, although he never became fluent in it. Nonetheless, the anime producers honored his ideals by making Esperanto the official written language of the film.

Reactions to the Anime

Similar to the original narration, symbolism, and imagery of Miyazawa's novella, the anime is quiet, even silent at times, gently slow-paced, with thoughtful, dreamlike qualities. Live birds turn into candy that the characters can eat as if that were completely normal. Fragrant red apples appear out of nowhere for children to share. Anime expert Justin Sevakis says the film is "as much

Kenji Miyazawa's Ongoing Influence

Kenji Miyazawa died more than ninety years ago. Yet his works frequently show up—sometimes as passing references, other times in more substantive ways—in contemporary anime and manga. The most famous anime inspired by Miyazawa's work is Leiji Matsumoto's *Galaxy Express 999* (a series that ran from 1977 through the early 2000s). Inspired by the imagery of a steam locomotive traveling through space from *Night on the Galactic Railroad*, Matsumoto created a popular series of science-fiction stories with intertwined characters who travel across the universe on an interstellar train. *Giovanni's Island* (2014) by Mizuho Nishikubo tells the story of two young Japanese boys on a Soviet-occupied island at the end of World War II. The boys love Miyazawa's novel, nicknaming themselves Giovanni and Campanella as they make frequent references to the parallels of their life story and the novel. The anime television series *Penguindrum* (2011–2012) refers to one of the stories from *Night on the Galactic Railroad* and also echoes his theme of self-sacrifice for the good of others. The anime *Flower and Asura* (2025) centers on a schoolgirl who loves reciting Miyazawa's poems and writings, while its opening and closing animations use images from *Night on the Galactic Railroad*.

of an enigma as I can imagine any anime has been. . . . It's slow and lyrical, but for those who are patient and introspective, it's one of the most deeply moving and compelling stories ever put to animation."[4] Ultimately, the novella and anime are both about second chances. Through the death of his friend, Giovanni learns that the true purpose of life is to bring happiness to those around him, and he commits himself to that goal.

Because of the deep philosophical and Buddhist spiritual themes of the novella, *Night on the Galactic Railroad* is considered to be one of the most culturally Japanese anime films ever made. It won the Ōfuji Noburō Award for animation in 1985 in recognition of its artistic achievement. As one of the first anime films released on American home video in the 1990s, it helped establish anime's reputation in the United States as something beautiful and distinct from American animated films and television series.

CHAPTER TWO

Osamu Tezuka and *Astro Boy*

Born in 1928 to a wealthy family in Toyonaka near the city of Osaka, Osamu Tezuka was raised in a home that emphasized arts and culture. Tezuka was an avid reader of the manga serials that were featured in Japanese magazines of the time. He was also a devoted fan of cartoons. His father had purchased a French-made film projector so he could show his family and neighbors the new foreign films and cartoons. Growing up, Tezuka watched Disney cartoons, including Mickey Mouse and Donald Duck shorts, and Fleischer cartoons, including *Betty Boop* and *Popeye*. He also enjoyed the *Felix the Cat* cartoons and the Chinese animated feature *Princess Iron Fan*. He was a huge fan of Disney's works, once claiming he had watched *Bambi* more than eighty times. Tezuka started drawing at an early age, and by junior high school he was making his own manga.

In 1944 he was sent to a boarding school for teenaged boys. Tezuka and his fellow students underwent rigorous training to toughen them up physically until they were old enough to join the military to fight for Japan in World War II. He graduated from high school in April 1945. He then enrolled as a medical student at Osaka University, so he avoided immediate military service. Four months later, Japan surrendered, and Tezuka could finally reveal his disgust for the war and his idealistic hopes for a better future. Soon after the US occupation of Japan started, however,

manga-ka
Japanese term for artists who create comic books and graphic novels

he was beaten up by some American soldiers. Tezuka believes this happened because, with his limited English, he did not understand what they were saying to him. As anime scholar Helen Mc-Carthy explains, "He began to wonder how people who didn't understand one another could ever be at peace. This [question] became one of the enduring themes of his work."[5]

Birth of Modern Manga

Tezuka attended medical school from 1945 through 1950, and while he studied intently, he was also involved in student musicals and performances as well as drawing manga on the side. His first published work was a comic strip for children in the *Mainichi* newspaper that premiered on New Year's Day 1946. He produced several short-run comic strips during medical school and published a full-length manga book, *New Treasure Island*, which features an adventure story based on an outline given him by another *manga-ka*, Shichima Sakai. Loosely inspired by Robert Louis Stevenson's classic novel *Treasure Island*, this manga is an updated version in which a young boy, Pete, finds a treasure map and races against pirates to find the valuables first.

The next year by chance, Tezuka saw a still photo of the female robot featured in Fritz Lang's 1927 groundbreaking science-fiction movie *Metropolis*. While the film is based on a

Osamu Tezuka (pictured in an undated photo) went to medical school but ultimately became the most popular and in-demand manga artist in Japan. His work revolutionized modern manga as an artform.

science-fiction novel and screenplay written by Thea von Harbou, Tezuka had not seen the movie or read the story. Yet from this single image, he imagined and created a complex, 160-page epic science-fiction manga, which he also called *Metropolis*.

art deco
An early twentieth-century style of art and architecture that features zigzags, geometric shapes, and ziggurat patterns

Tezuka's version, published in 1949, is set in a modern urban near-future at a time when the sun is experiencing extraordinary and dangerous sunspot activity. The manga's background scenes feature remarkable art deco–inspired architecture, similar to the cityscapes of early twentieth-century Chicago and New York City. The story focuses on the power struggles and conflict of politics, society, and technology, centered on the creation of an artificial humanoid life form. The manga became popular beyond anyone's expectations and provided definitive evidence that manga could be regarded as serious literature. The success of Tezuka's *Metropolis* also encouraged numerous young artists to aspire to write and draw manga. By the time Tezuka finished medical school, his early manga experience helped him land a job with a Tokyo manga magazine to produce the series known in the United States as *Kimba the White Lion*. So in 1951 he decided to leave medicine to become a full-time manga-ka.

Growing Fame

Tezuka went on to become the most popular and in-demand manga-ka in Japan. His work revolutionized modern manga as an art form in Japan. Drawing on his skills as a storyteller and the cinematic staging of his artwork (which he had developed through his love of film), he infused a new energy and liveliness into the world of manga. He was soon busy running several stories in several different magazines. When editors could not hire him to work for their magazine, they would ask for someone whose work resembled Tezuka's style. This led many other manga-ka to imitate his style, particularly the signature big eyes of his characters.

In a sense, all modern manga-ka since the 1950s are followers and descendants of Tezuka, which is why he has been given the nickname of the "god" or "father of manga."

After World War II Japan struggled to return to its prior prosperity. Most families had little money for anything other than essentials. The rise of manga at this time came about because comics printed on cheap paper were an affordable form of fun, so an entire generation of Japanese children grew up with manga as their primary source of entertainment. Keiji Nakazawa, the manga-ka who created the award-winning manga *Barefoot Gen* about his experiences after the bombing of Hiroshima, describes how important manga reading was for him back then. As McCarthy writes, Nakazawa remembers reading Tezuka's *New Treasure Island* while "living in the burnt-out ruins of Hiroshima with his mother and being riveted to the adventure."[6]

In 1952 Tezuka began what was to become his signature work. *Astro Boy* is the story of an atomic-powered robot boy who fights for peace and justice. As the only country ever to have

Pluto

Although Tezuka died in 1989, one of his works made a comeback in the twenty-first century. From 2003 to 2009 the manga-ka Naoki Urasawa wrote and illustrated a manga series called *Pluto* that reworked "The Greatest Robot on Earth" story arc from Tezuka's *Astro Boy* manga, turning it into a darker and more nuanced conflict. In Tezuka's story a robot named Pluto, who was created to be the king of all robots, sets out to destroy the seven strongest robots, including Astro Boy. In *Pluto*, the main character is a robot detective working for a fictitious European police agency called Europol. That character, named Gesicht, tries to stop Pluto from carrying out his plan. Astro Boy only enters the story in the second half and ultimately has the final confrontation with Pluto.

Pluto echoes many of Tezuka's themes, including triumphing over hatred and the question of what it means to be truly human in a world dominated by machines and artificial intelligence. The manga has won numerous awards, including being named one of the Great Graphic Novels for Teens by the American Library Association in 2009. An anime version made and broadcast worldwide on Netflix in 2023 instantly brought the story to a larger audience.

nuclear weapons used on it, Japan has a complicated relationship with atomic power. The *Godzilla* films (starting in 1954) represent a primal and violent response to the threat of annihilation. By contrast, Tezuka's manga series represent a more intellectual reaction, which resonated strongly with the Japanese imagination at the time. As McCarthy explains, "*Astro Boy* is the sum of Tezuka's background, influences, experiences, and belief. . . . Astro is a typical Tezuka juvenile lead, wanting to do good, but unsure what good is. . . . *Astro Boy* is not a hymn to technology, but a warning that science alone cannot solve the problems humanity creates."[7]

Entering the World of Animation

From the time he watched cartoons as a child, Tezuka dreamed of creating animations himself. After his success in manga, he founded an animation studio, Mushi Production, in 1961. The rise of television opened a new avenue for anime, but it also presented challenges. Television demanded more hours of animation than movies did, but television companies could only pay for a fraction of the cost of production. To successfully produce what TV anime required, Tezuka needed a way to create more animation for a lower cost per minute. Drawing on the ideas coming from TV animations made in the United States (notably Hanna-Barbera cartoons), he decided to adopt a limited animation style. Most movies of the time ran at twenty-four frames per second, repeating each image twice so there were twelve images drawn for each second of film. With the limited animation technique, Tezuka cut the number of animated images needed down to eight or even four per second, which saved labor time and costs. To further cut costs, the production team emphasized scenes in which a character would freeze in a pose for a second or more, and they frequently recycled scenes from episode to episode.

limited animation
A money-saving and labor-saving style of animation that uses fewer drawings per second of film and freeze-frames to lower production costs

Osamu Tezuka's many beloved characters are here seen pointing the way to a Kyoto mini museum devoted to Tezuka's art. His best-known character, Astro Boy, stands at the front of the group.

Even with these cost-cutting measures, Tezuka still had to underprice Mushi Production's work to sell it to the networks. To make a profit, they relied instead on merchandizing and commercial sponsorships. On New Year's Day 1963, the animated version of *Astro Boy* premiered on Japanese television. It was so popular that it was soon sold to the United States, where in September 1963 it became the first anime broadcast on US television. Despite this success, the series barely earned enough to recoup the costs of producing it. As anime scholar Jonathan Clements writes, "Only a year after *Astro Boy*'s TV debut, Tezuka was already privately admitting that Mushi was following a 'dangerous business model.'"[8]

Despite these business challenges, Tezuka continued with his ambitious projects. He created a wide variety of manga, anime, and feature films between the 1960s and the 1980s. When his studio Mushi Production went bankrupt in 1973, he formed a new animation studio, Tezuka Productions. Many of the animators and directors who worked for him at Mushi Production went on to become major figures in the anime industry.

Later Works

Tezuka also continued creating extended manga serials, most notably *Buddha* (1972–1983) and *Phoenix* (1967–1988). *Buddha* retells the story of the life of Siddhartha Gautama (aka the Buddha), with Tezuka inserting his trademark comic and action elements, yet remaining faithful and respectful to the central spiritual teachings of Buddhism. Tezuka considered *Phoenix* to be his life's work and was planning more installments of it at the time of his death in February 1989. *Phoenix* consists of twelve story arcs, each centered on the themes of life, death, and the belief that all life is valuable. The stories stretch across time from the mythical past of 350 BCE to a science-fiction future of the thirty-fifth century.

The Lion King Controversy

Besides *Astro Boy*, the other well-known Tezuka anime series that was broadcast on US television was *Kimba the White Lion*. The 1966 production was based on the manga he drew in the early 1950s. In the manga and the television series, Kimba was a lion cub and orphan son of the king of the jungle. The cub is cared for by humans and returns to the wild to build a community of wild animals who live in harmony with people.

When Disney released its animated feature *The Lion King* in 1994, people in the anime and manga communities in both Japan and the United States noted similarities between the Disney and Tezuka stories. Some said it appeared that Disney had stolen the plot from Tezuka's story. While there were several general similarities in the characters, there were significant differences between the two storylines, and the Tezuka family did not pursue any litigation. In general, however, the Japanese opinion was that Disney should at least acknowledge some inspiration from *Kimba the White Lion*. Citing legal and financial reasons, Disney did not admit to any outside creative inspiration.

Japan considers Tezuka and his works to be a national treasure. In 1989 the Japanese government posthumously honored him with the Order of the Sacred Treasure (equivalent to the US Presidential Medal of Freedom) for his lifetime's work. In 1997 the Japanese post office issued commemorative stamps of Tezuka and his characters. Much of this work is collected and displayed at the Osamu Tezuka Manga Museum in Takarazuka, Japan.

No other single person has had as much influence over the course of manga and anime as Osamu Tezuka has. During his lifetime he produced over 170,000 pages of manga covering more than seven hundred different titles. His lifelong devotion to his art resulted in a lasting legacy of visual storytelling techniques and new industry standards that made the modern phenomena of anime and manga possible. Legend has it that his last words were, "I'm begging you, let me work."[9]

CHAPTER THREE

Hayao Miyazaki and *Nausicaä of the Valley of the Wind*

Hayao Miyazaki is currently the most famous anime creator in the world. Many also consider him the greatest animator of all time. Since cofounding Studio Ghibli in 1985, he has been recognized as the world's most accomplished and influential anime writer and director. In addition to many anime shorts, he has written and directed a dozen full-length anime, including *My Neighbor Totoro*, *Kiki's Delivery Service*, *Princess Mononoke*, and *Howl's Moving Castle*. His works have won global acclaim and over one hundred awards. His creative impact on animation and film has been honored with numerous lifetime achievement awards, and two of his films, *Spirited Away* (2001) and *The Boy and the Heron* (2024), have won Academy Awards for Best Animated Feature.

Born January 5, 1941, in Tokyo City, Japan, Miyazaki grew up in a well-off family, yet he still experienced emotional and economic stresses during World War II. At the young age of three or four, he formed vivid memories of bombed-out neighborhoods and the fearful feeling of fleeing a safe home during evacuations. Perhaps because his father and uncle ran a factory that built parts for Japanese fighter planes, he spent a lot of time drawing warplanes, battleships, and tanks. Unlike other school-age boys who were obsessed with the potential war power of giant fantasy robots, Miyazaki's fascination with the nuts-and-bolts level of things reflected his belief that ingenious flying machines and adaptable vehicles could help humans achieve bigger and better things. This feeling is reflected in the nineteenth-century steam-power-inspired steampunk style that he uses to depict technology from windmills, gliders, and broken-down airplanes to a clunky, funky castle that walks on chicken's legs.

steampunk
An artistic and cultural style inspired by nineteenth-century Industrial Revolution steam-powered machines and gadgets

Influences and Inspirations

Like many others, Miyazaki was influenced by the work of Osamu Tezuka. As a young artist, he created and discarded thousands of pages of manga because they seemed too similar to Tezuka's style. Miyazaki tried to respectfully admire and learn from Tezuka's work while developing his own unique artistry.

Hayao Miyazaki is the most famous—and many would say, greatest—anime creator in the world. His works, including the Academy Award–winning films Spirited Away *and* The Boy and the Heron, *have won global acclaim.*

gekiga
"Dramatic pictures" in Japanese, referring to manga comics with dark imagery, criminal violence, and mature themes

Another powerful inspiration for Miyazaki was the first full-color feature-length anime created in Japan. That 1958 film, *Legend of the White Snake*, is based on a Chinese legend of a young man who encounters an enchanted snake that can take the form of a beautiful maiden. At the time it premiered, Miyazaki was in his last year of high school and feeling exhausted from the demands of studying for college entrance exams. Along with other anxious students, he had been obsessively reading popular *gekiga* manga, which focus on humanity's dark side and tend to be depressing, gritty, dramatic, and violent.

Legend of the White Snake changed the course of Miyazaki's life. When he first saw the film, he told the audience attending one of his lectures, he immediately "fell in love with the heroine . . . and was moved to the depths of [his] soul" as her noble character and dedication seemed to restore his faith in humanity. He also fell in love with the medium, which made manga art move and come to life. He already knew that he wanted to draw for a living, but now he saw a way to break out of his doom and gloom and create art with a positive purpose. The film, he said, "made me realize how stupid I was. It made me realize that, behind a façade of cynical pronouncements, in actuality I really was in love with the pure, earnest world of the film. . . . I was no longer able to deny the fact that there was another me—a me that yearned desperately to affirm the world rather than negate it."[10]

Starting Point

For the first twenty years of his career, Miyazaki worked at various studios on numerous anime television series and feature films. At first he provided basic drawings for anime, and later he created storyboards and scene designs and began codirecting. Although Miyazaki gained experience in many phases of the animation industry during these formative years, he found the process tedious

Miyazaki's Mentor, Isao Takahata

When Miyazaki worked as a junior animator at Tōei Animation in 1963, Isao Takahata was his senior mentor (*sempai*, in Japanese). Takahata worked primarily as a screenwriter and producer, not as an animator. The two worked collaboratively on several early projects, such as *Panda! Go, Panda!* and *Lupin III*. Although they had very different personalities and often argued, their creative differences made each of them better. According to their mutual mentor, Yasuo Ōtsuka, Takahata encouraged Miyazaki to develop a sense of social responsibility in his artistic productions and urged him to focus on anime more than manga comics. When Miyazaki directed the anime of *Nausicaä of the Valley of the Wind* (1984), Takahata served as producer.

Following the film's success, they were able to form Studio Ghibli, where they could continue to make animated films in the way they thought best. Though Miyazaki has made most of the best-known Ghibli films, Takahata directed and wrote (or cowrote) five feature films for the studio, including *Grave of the Fireflies* (1988), *Pom Poko* (1994), and *The Tale of Princess Kaguya* (2013). Collectively, their creative conflicts and challenges helped produce some of the most highly acclaimed works in anime history.

and unfulfilling. It seemed to him that the studio's primary goal was making a profit rather than exploring ways to use the artistry of images and words to create stories of lasting beauty and meaning. Miyazaki believed that manga could express complex human feelings and help people think and feel their way through difficult times and dilemmas.

Miyazaki's belief in the creative potential of this visual storytelling form was so strong that even in the middle of other projects he continued to make time to write and draw manga. In early works such as *People of the Desert* and *Shuna's Journey*, Miyazaki tested out his own ideas about manga storytelling. These ideas included using words and images to build complex imaginary worlds where the natural environment, plants, animals, and humans must learn to understand each other, resolve crises, and find ways to live in harmony. Many of the natural settings, characters, and plotlines that he experimented with in these early manga helped him create the epic *Nausicaä of the Valley of the Wind*, which is now considered his masterwork and a world-class masterpiece of visual storytelling.

Nausicaä in Print

Although many fans may only know *Nausicaä* as an anime, the full storyline originated as a long-running manga. Both forms of *Nausicaä of the Valley of the Wind* center on the adventures of a young princess who lives in a postapocalyptic future in which humanity is dying and the natural world is covered by poisonous forests inhabited by giant insects. Many of the remaining humans believe that the insects and forests are the problem so they try to destroy them. But, by exploring and studying the wasteland, Nausicaä learns that humans have it all wrong: the forests are actually cleansing the pollution caused by previous generations, not causing it. The people of the world must then learn to overcome their us-versus-them

Origin of the Character of Nausicaä

Nausicaä is not a Japanese name, so where did the character and her name come from? The original Nausicaä was a princess of the island kingdom of Phaeacia near Greece and appears in Homer's epic poem *The Odyssey*. When Odysseus was shipwrecked on the island, Nausicaä and her handmaids discovered him on the beach. She rescued him and arranged for her parents to allow him to stay until he was well enough to continue his journey.

Miyazaki once explained that he had read a description of her as "a beautiful and fanciful girl . . . [who] took delight in nature and had an especially sensitive personality." This account reminded him of an aristocratic young girl from a tenth-century Japanese folktale known as "the princess who loved insects." Instead of being interested in the court fashions and romantic affairs, she was fascinated by insects and devoted herself to studying them. The two princesses became a single person in Miyazaki's mind, and together they formed the Nausicaä of the manga and anime.

Hayao Miyazaki, *Nausicaä of the Valley of the Wind*, vol. 1, 2nd ed. San Francisco: VIZ Media, 2004, back flyleaf.

mentality and work with each other and the forests in order to restore some balance to their relationship with the natural world.

Miyazaki's masterpiece was born partly by chance and partly out of necessity. Near the end of 1981, the editor of the new *Animage* magazine, Toshio Suzuki, invited him to develop an original manga. Since he then had no other paying work lined up, Miyazaki agreed, but had one condition: that the manga must never be made into an anime. In his view, he explained, manga and anime are two separate forms of art and storytelling: "If I draw a comic, I draw something not meant to be animated. Otherwise, there would be no meaning for me in what I do. Nothing can be less interesting than a comic that has been drawn with the hidden intention of turning it into a movie. Although there are lots of comics like that, they are inferior products. A comic book is a comic book. It's different from a movie."[11] For the special story he had in mind, Miyazaki wanted to focus intensely on creating rich visual storytelling art and not be distracted by wondering how to pitch it as an animated series or film.

tankobon

The Japanese word for "stand-alone book"; in English, the term refers to a collection of manga serials bound together and sold in multivolume sets, so all of the episodes of the manga can be read as one complete narrative

Once Suzuki agreed to these terms, Miyazaki began drawing the complex images for the story, working primarily in pencil. The manga was then printed in monochrome sepia-toned ink, which highlighted the distinct artwork of each page. The story's setting and plot were influenced by actual ecological disasters (such as the mid-twentieth-century mercury contamination of Japan's Minamata Bay) and scientific studies of the history of agriculture. Other influences included literary epics such as Homer's *Odyssey*, Frank Herbert's *Dune*, works by J.R.R Tolkien, and eco-science fiction. The first installment appeared in February 1982, and the series ran for over twelve years. When it was later reprinted in seven *tankobon* volumes, the complete work spanned 1,060 pages and sold more than 10 million copies in its first two years.

Nausicaä on the Screen

The *Nausicaä* manga became so popular so quickly that Suzuki soon broke his promise and asked Miyazaki to adapt it into an anime. Miyazaki resisted. One problem was that the art style he had used was so detailed and visually dense that he could not imagine simplifying it (and he did not really want to). Another issue was that he had not yet introduced all of the characters and plot elements that he thought were essential, so there was no end to the story in sight. The anime, he knew, would require a strong ending. Years later, Miyazaki recalled that the dilemma felt even worse because his manga story featured a female hero caught up in multiple layers of cultural and ecological crises that paralleled real-world environmental and world problems that no one, including himself, had any idea how to solve. To complete the manga, he once said, he would have "to write what he did not know,"[12] and that could not happen in time to inspire the anime's conclusion.

Nausicaä of the Valley of the Wind *started out as a manga. The manga and later anime (pictured) both center on the adventures of a young princess who lives in a postapocalyptic future filled with poisonous forests, giant insects, and little hope for humanity.*

By 1984, however, Miyazaki had managed to adapt selected elements from the first sixteen chapters of the manga into a full-length anime feature. The fine visual details of his imaginative artwork truly came to life in the beautifully refined color palette on the big screen, but he only gave himself a grade of 65 out of 100 for the ending.

The Birth of Studio Ghibli

Although Miyazaki complained that the adaptation process was agony and almost drove him insane, the anime succeeded both artistically and financially. Its success led to the 1985 creation of the now-renowned anime company Studio Ghibli. As Japanese culture writer Alicia Haddick explains, "The success of *Nausicaä* allowed the trio of Suzuki, Miyazaki and Takahata—skeleton, brain and heart—to form the body of the Studio Ghibli we know and love today. The new studio offered the space and, with profits from their movies and sponsors willing to help fund original productions, the freedom . . . to follow their passions and create almost anything they wanted."[13]

Miyazaki continued to write the *Nausicaä* manga for another ten years, stopping at intervals to work on many of Studio Ghibli's most-beloved anime. From beginning to end, the manga's story of environmental collapse grows increasingly complex, darker, and more grim.

The long experience of creating the complex world of the *Nausicaä* manga uniquely shaped Miyazaki's development as a serious storyteller, imaginative visual world-builder, anime creator, and successful studio director. Over the course of his life and career, Miyazaki's manga and anime works have offered millions of readers and viewers invaluable ways to feel and think about how to live.

CHAPTER FOUR

Yoshiyuki Tomino and *Mobile Suit Gundam*

Born in 1941 during World War II, Yoshiyuki Tomino is the son of an engineer and the grandson of a toy manufacturer. That heritage seemed to foretell his future as the creator of a major giant-robot, or *mecha*, series and the most popular line of model-kit robots in the world. He acquired his interest in science and engineering from his father but failed when he applied for admission to a technical high school. Instead, he attended a regular high school, where he focused on the humanities. Growing up in 1950s Japan, he became a fan of both foreign and Japanese science-fictions films, so for college he chose to study filmmaking at Nihon University College of Art in Tokyo.

After he graduated in the early 1960s, Tomino went to work at Mushi Production, Osamu Tezuka's animation studio. There he worked in the production department, learning the process of animation from his interactions with the animators. He later worked on writing episodes of Tezuka's *Astro Boy* anime TV series and doing storyboards for the animators. In 1972 several members of Mushi left to form Sunrise Studio, and Tomino joined them. Together they worked on numerous anime throughout the 1970s, including many classic mecha anime such as *Zero Tester*, *Brave Reideen*, *Combattler V*, *Voltes V*, and *Future Robot Daltanious*. Tomino was the cocreator of one of these shows, *Invincible Super Man Zambot 3*. These anime were simple action-adventure shows aimed at children.

They featured heroes piloting giant robots built by scientists to battle aliens or other robots and save humankind. Tomino's passion for the technical sophistication of the engineering design of robots and other mechanical devices is clearly demonstrated through the attention to detail he presented in these shows.

storyboards
In anime, typically hand-drawn comic panels that show the key scenes, character designs, and plot turning points that will be used in creating the film; they often include director's instructions, important dialogue, and brief backstory descriptions

Revolution in Giant Robot Anime

In the late 1970s Tomino was given an opportunity to write and direct a new robot show, but he wanted to do something different. As he told an interviewer, he felt that giant robot anime shows were too simplistic, showing only one side of a conflict as if that were the only side that mattered. "Most of the war-related dramas and movies were quite one-sided, described from one perspective. However, war is something where millions of people meet and fight each other, each believing in justice on their own sides. Mecha anime tends to be one-sided, but considering war objectively, I thought I should describe war from both sides."[14] The result was *Mobile Suit Gundam*, a 1979 TV series that changed the direction of anime.

The series takes place in a distant future, ostensibly set in the year 0079 of the Universal Century—a time that is seventy-nine years after humans started colonizing space. Some of the space colonies have banded together, calling themselves the Principality of Zeon. Together they have declared political independence from the Earth Federation and are fighting a war in space with the Earth forces. The two sides fight with human-piloted robots called mobile suits. Amuro

mecha
In general, mechanical robots, tanks, jets, submarines, and so forth; or more specifically, mechanical robots that are piloted by human (or humanoid) pilots from within a cockpit

Ray is a young mechanic who lives in an Earth Federation colony. His father is the leader of a project to develop an advanced secret fighting robot called the RX-78 Gundam for the Earth Federation. Just as a Federation ship arrives to pick up the robot, a surprise attack on the colony by two Zeon mobile suit pilots kills Amuro's father. Despite his lack of training, Amuro is able to pilot the Gundam and use its advanced capabilities to defeat the two Zeon mobile suits. Amuro is able to do this because he possesses an almost supernatural mental awareness that bonds him directly with the robot, a newly evolved form of human known as a newtype. Seeing that he is a natural pilot, a Federation officer assigns Amuro to pilot the

Yoshiyuki Tomino (pictured in 2024 with his RX-78-2 Gundam) believed that most giant robot anime was too one-sided. His 1979 Mobile Suit Gundam *series showed both sides of a conflict—and in the process, changed the direction of anime.*

What Is a Franchise?

Star Trek started as a single TV series in 1967, and *Star Wars* started as a single movie in 1977, but both spawned a series of sequels, prequels, and other series, movies, cartoons, and novels all set in the same fictional universe. Frequently the main characters from the original work will appear in the follow-on works, and some of them are even set in an alternative universe that is different from the original setting.

In the entertainment industry this is called a franchise. *Gundam* has become a highly popular franchise with over sixty anime TV series, movies, direct to video animations, and novels, as well as over eighty video games. Tomino personally created seven of these follow-on series and movies and has been at least partially involved in almost all of them. By any measure *Gundam* is the most successful entertainment franchise to come out of Japan.

Gundam. Thus begins the war between the Principality of Zeon, led by the charismatic Char Aznable, and the Earth Federation.

Mobile Suit Gundam ran for forty-three episodes and traced out the convoluted story of the war with a large cast of characters fighting (and often being killed) in the battles. Tomino showed the stories and motivations of the characters of both sides, demonstrating that each thought they were battling on the side of righteousness. His intended purpose was to show that ultimately war is ambiguous, stupid, and evil—that everyone is harmed, even those who feel that their cause is justified. The battles between Amuro and Char, who become bitter rivals, are always one-on-one in the style of classic samurai warriors fighting each other according to a code of honor. It is for this reason that the Gundams are consciously designed to look like samurai armor turned into battle robots.

Model Robots

Presenting a complex story of conflict rather than the one-dimensional good guys versus alien invaders of the previous giant robot anime came at a price. The show did not get high ratings and was almost canceled after thirty-nine episodes. It was saved by its merchandising. The Bandai toy company purchased the rights to sell plastic models of the various Gundam and other mobile suits. Called Gunpla (a combination of *Gundam* and *plastic*), these inexpensive models proved to be wildly popular. Since 1980 Bandai has produced over one thousand different models of Gunpla and sold nearly 1 billion of them worldwide.

The Gunpla sparked a renewed interest in *Mobile Suit Gundam*, and the ratings improved when it was rebroadcast. During this second run, it was successful enough that Tomino was able to make a follow-on series, *Mobile Suit Zeta Gundam*, that debuted in 1985. The new series explored the events that followed the war as new factions form and new fights break out. After this, Tomino made a feature film, *Mobile Suit Gundam: Char's Counterattack*. In that film, which premiered in 1988, the rivalry between Amuro and Char reaches a climax that involves saving the Earth from an asteroid collision.

Growing a Franchise

After this movie, Sunrise Studio used the popularity of the franchise to make more *Gundam* series and films with different directors and writers leading the projects. Some of the stories follow

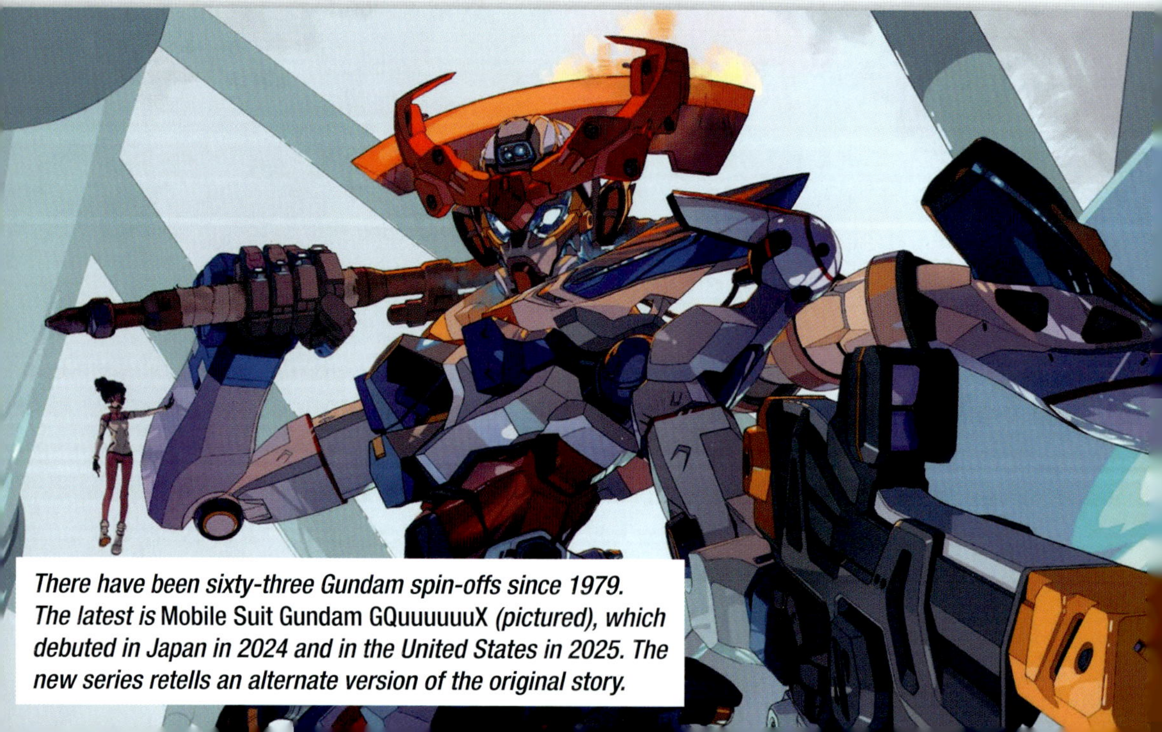

There have been sixty-three Gundam spin-offs since 1979. The latest is Mobile Suit Gundam GQuuuuuuX *(pictured), which debuted in Japan in 2024 and in the United States in 2025. The new series retells an alternate version of the original story.*

Gundam and Space Colonization

As the popularity of mecha anime shows increased throughout the 1970s, so did the general public's interest in the real possibility of building space colonies. At that time a group of scientists led by Princeton University physicist Gerard K. O'Neill began mapping out ideas and designs for building space colonies inhabited by thousands of people. The colonies would be built using material mined from the moon, while further mining and manufacturing would enable a large-scale migration of over 1 million humans into near-Earth space. Tomino read the research papers and books published by this group and used their intriguing ideas as inspiration for his development of the *Mobile Suit Gundam* universe. He adapted O'Neill's cylinder-shaped space colony design into many of his fictional colonies. In O'Neill's design, two nested cylindrical structures rotate in opposite directions to (theoretically) keep it aimed toward the sun and create artificial gravity for inhabitants inside. Tomino specifically used this design as the basis for his Island Three space colony.

the original timeline and are set in the Universal Century of the original series, while others play with alternative *Gundam* narratives set in various other timelines. Since 1979 there have been sixty-three different TV series or films spun off of the *Gundam* story. The most recent series is *Mobile Suit Gundam GQuuuuuuX*, which debuted in Japan in 2024 and in the United States in 2025. This latest series retells an alternative version of the original story. It is designed to appeal to both the old-school *Gundam* fans and the new generation who are now the grandchildren of the original fans from 1979.

Uniting all of the *Gundam* stories is Tomino's ideal that anime should be about something more than just action. This is why the show continues to deal with themes of justice, the responsibility of people to each other, economic inequality, political corruption, the dangers humans pose to the environment, and even social gender roles. For example, *Mobile Suit Gundam: The Witch from Mercury* (2022) was the first *Gundam* story to feature an LGBTQ protagonist. Not all of Tomino's serious messages, however, seem to reach the fans. In a 2022 interview, Tomino expressed frustration that many viewers do not pick up on the deeper themes and issues he has presented in the various series. “They [the viewers] don’t expect anime to deal with theories of civilization and culture. It’s only anime after all.”[15]

Over the forty-five years since *Gundam* first premiered, the various series and movies have come to define modern anime of the twentieth and twenty-first centuries. Despite Tomino’s words to the contrary, most *Gundam* fans have picked up and taken his ideas and themes to heart. *Gundam* has shown that it is more than simple action-adventure stories for their own sake, instead demonstrating that anime can take on and present serious themes and ideas to audiences.

CHAPTER FIVE

Riyoko Ikeda and *The Rose of Versailles*

When the modern manga industry started in Japan after World War II, essentially all the manga-ka were men. That situation began to change in the early 1970s with the arrival of the so-called Year 24 Group. Though not an organized group, this was the label given to about a dozen female manga-ka who entered the industry at about the same time. All were born in or around 1949, known as *Shōwa 24* on the Japanese calendar.

One of these women was Riyoko Ikeda, born in Osaka in 1947. She attended college to study philosophy and originally hoped to become a scholar or university professor. Her father, however, disapproved of girls studying and would only pay for one year of tuition. She had artistic talent, so she decided to take up drawing manga to earn a living and to pay for her further education. In 1967 she published her first manga, *The Maiden of the Rose Mansion*. The shōjo (girls') manga story revolves around a young girl who narrates the history of her older brother's tragic love of a beautiful girl who dies of cancer.

shōjo
A type of manga in which the storylines, character designs, and art style are specifically created to appeal to young girl (shōjo) readers

Looking Back at the French Revolution

In the late 1960s, protests at universities in Japan and around the world caused students to become more politically aware.

Year 24 Group

A cohort of female manga-ka who are collectively credited with ushering in the golden age of shōjo manga during the 1970s by expanding conventional comedy-romance storylines and introducing more serious and mature themes

As a college student, Ikeda became involved, studying politics and questioning Japan's traditional norms and strict societal roles. Through the 1960s, shōjo manga focused mainly on an elementary schoolgirl audience with innocuous romance stories. With the arrival of the Year 24 manga-ka, shōjo manga began branching out into science fiction, historical fiction, political themes, and same-sex romance with androgynous characters. Having been fascinated with Marie Antoinette and the French Revolution as a high school student, Ikeda persuaded her all-male board of editors at Margaret Comics to publish a manga about this era. *The Rose of Versailles* began its serialization on May 21, 1972. The choice of this subject was no accident. According to scholar Nobuko Anan, Ikeda "wanted the French Revolution in this manga to symbolize 'the inner revolution of the Japanese women' in the age when they could not choose their own lives."[16]

Riyoko Ikeda's fascination with Marie Antoinette and the French Revolution led her to create The Rose of Versailles *manga. With her characters in the background, Ikeda welcomes visitors to a 2022 Tokyo art museum exhibit of her work.*

Rose of Versailles Onstage

The Takarazuka Revue is an all-women musical stage company that is over one hundred years old. Its long-running popularity is based on creating shows that cater to a female audience and featuring romantic drama and *bishōnen* (beautiful boy) leading characters played by female actors. Consequently, it was a natural fit for the company to stage a musical production of *The Rose of Versailles*, and it proved highly successful. The original production was staged in 1974 with over thirty variations of the story and music performed either at the home theater in Takarazuka (near Osaka), Japan, or as road shows through 2024.

The Rose of Versailles manga focuses on two main characters, the historical figure of Marie Antoinette, queen of France and wife to King Louis XVI, and the fictional character of Oscar François de Jarjayes, a young woman who was the head of the Royal Guard protecting the queen. The story of Marie Antoinette as the last queen of France is well known, but Ikeda made the story fresh by relating that history through the eyes of Oscar. Born into nobility herself, Oscar is the daughter of a nobleman and member of the Royal Guard who wanted a male heir to succeed him. But when his wife dies in childbirth, he gives his newborn daughter a male name and raises her as if she were a boy, dressing her as male and training her in swordsmanship and military fighting techniques. At age fourteen, Oscar is sent (along with her childhood friend and servant, André Grandier) to the palace. There she serves as the head of the Royal Guard of Marie Antoinette, who is newly arrived at court, just prior to her marriage to Louis XVI. Oscar becomes the confidant to the young queen as the story covers the twenty-year period from her arrival in 1769 to the start of the French Revolution in 1789. Although Oscar is open about the fact that she is female, throughout the story she is allowed all the societal freedom and status that the conventional male head of the guard would receive. Her freedom starkly contrasts to that allowed other women in the queen's circle.

The storyline follows two main tracks. The familiar historical one shows Marie Antoinette becoming the victim of palace intrigue and the symbol of a royal who is blind to the suffering of the commoners. The second is a fictional history in which Oscar, through her love of André, becomes more aware of the injustices of the royal system and expresses sympathy for the plight of commoners like André. Torn between her love for André and her obligation to serve her queen, Oscar eventually leaves the Royal Guard to join the revolutionaries. She dies heroically during the storming of the Bastille, the 1789 event that became the symbol of revolutionary struggle. The anime ends with Marie Antoinette being deposed by revolutionaries and ultimately sentenced to death by guillotine. As anime experts Jonathan Clements and Helen McCarthy write, "The two deaths are very different. Oscar's is a triumph of the human spirit, Antoinette's a failure . . . the proud, brave Antoinette has colluded in the lies and injustice that made the revolution inevitable . . . [but] in finally rejecting a system that separates people with artificial barriers of rank and property, Oscar asserts her own right to be fully human, regardless of gender or status."[17]

Popular Success and Move to Television

The manga serial was an immediate hit, running until the fall of 1973 for eighty-two weekly chapters, which were then compiled into fourteen volumes of manga. While Marie Antoinette was the primary character at the start of the manga, Oscar grew in popularity with the readers as the series progressed. Ikeda responded to reader interest by expanding the character of Oscar. Anime

The Rose of Versailles in France

It is one thing for a show to be successful portraying French history in Japan, but how would the French react to this historical fiction? The French have long been fans of Japanese manga and anime, so the manga was translated and published in French in the early 1980s, while the anime was broadcast in France starting in 1986. There the fans enthusiastically welcomed both works, making Riyoko Ikeda famous in France. As a result, in 2008 she was awarded France's National Order of the Legion of Honour for raising awareness and appreciation of French culture in Japan through her manga.

Costumed fans surround The Rose of Versailles *creator Riyoko Ikeda at a publishing industry exhibition. The popularity of Ikeda's manga series has continued over time, spawning new manga as well as stage and film versions.*

scholar Susan J. Napier points out that "Ikeda actually changed the plot to emphasize Oscar more vividly because of strong reader response to the character. The interaction between fans and creators, with fan reaction affecting the development of a series, remains an important element in shōjo manga culture to this day."[18]

Because of the manga's popularity, a forty-episode TV anime series based on *The Rose of Versailles* was created by TMS Entertainment and broadcast on Nippon Television from October 1979 through September 1980. The anime version fulfilled the fans' desire to make Oscar the protagonist while Marie Antoinette became a supporting character. *The Rose of Versailles* became one of the most popular TV anime series of the early 1980s in Japan.

Revival in the 2020s

The proof of the power of *The Rose of Versailles* is its longevity. While most anime and manga serials are initially popular then fade after several years, *The Rose of Versailles* has remained popular in Japan for over fifty years, bringing in several new generations of fans. The story was adapted for the stage in 1974 and has been revived multiple times. Under the title *Lady Oscar*, it was the subject of a live-action film in 1979. The film was a Japanese-French coproduction filmed in English but was mainly shown to Japanese audiences. To celebrate the fiftieth anniversary of the initial publication of the manga, in 2022 an exhibition was held in Tokyo. On display were original artwork from the manga and the anime, along with costumes and props from the stage production. As part of the celebration, it was announced that a new anime feature film version of the story had started production. It was released in Japan in January 2025 and worldwide on Netflix in April 2025, thus allowing Oscar and her dreams of social equality to inspire the current generation of girls and fans worldwide.

Rumiko Takahashi and *Ranma ½*

Rumiko Takahashi has the distinction of being the richest manga-ka in the world. Creator of six major manga series and over a dozen shorter series and single-chapter manga, she is also now the most famous manga-ka in the world. Born in 1957, she grew up on the east coast of Japan in the Niigata Prefecture. As a young child, she did not have any strong desire to be an artist. It was not until she was in college that she started drawing manga as a hobby. She found further motivation when she took a short course at the Gekiga Sonjuku manga school, where she studied under the well-known manga-ka Kazuo Koike, creator of the manga *Lone Wolf and Cub*.

one-shot manga
Comic books or graphic novels that consist of a single chapter based on a stand-alone story arc

While she was in manga school, Takahashi published her first few works as *dōjinshi*, self-published comics generally sold at comic fairs attended by fans. In 1978 she won an honorable mention in the Shogakukan New Comics Contest for a one-shot manga called *Those Selfish Aliens* that was published in the contest sponsor's magazine, *Weekly Shōnen Sunday*. She expanded this story into the series *Urusei Yatsura* (*Those Obnoxious Aliens*), which began publication later in 1978 and quickly became a hit.

dōjinshi
Self-published comics generally sold at comic fairs attended by fans

Rumiko Takahashi (pictured in 2022) is the richest and most famous manga artist in the world. Her six major manga series and over a dozen shorter series and single-chapter manga have attracted a huge following and won critical acclaim.

Most manga-ka feel lucky to have one, or maybe two, hit series. In her career Takahashi has had six long-running hits: *Urusei Yatsura* (1978–1987), *Maison Ikkoku* (1980–1987), *Ranma ½* (1987–1996), *Inuyasha* (1996–2008), *Rin-ne* (2009–2017), and *Mao* (2019–). She has also created dozens of shorter series. When she ended her first two successful series in 1987, she started *Ranma ½*, a new comedy-action manga that attracted an even larger readership than both of her previous series.

Martial Arts Hijinks

Playing off the popularity of manga series that focused on martial arts, Takahashi's new series centered on sixteen-year-old Ranma Saotome, who was being trained as a martial artist by his father, Genma Saotome. When father and son travel to a Chinese training ground of water pools, because of his inability to read Chinese, Genma does not realize that each pool is tied to a supernatural curse. Ranma falls into the Pool of a Drowned Girl, while Genma falls into the Pool of a Drowned Panda. As a result, whenever they get wet, Ranma turns into a girl and Genma turns into a panda. Being doused with hot water turns them back into their original form.

The story begins as they arrive in Tokyo, where Genma's friend Soun Tendo owns a martial arts training center, or dojo. Genma and Soun had arranged for Ranma to marry one of Soun's three daughters and maintain the dojo. The two older sisters quickly decide that their tomboy youngest sister, Akane, who also is an accomplished martial artist and the same age as Ranma, should be his fiancée. It is hate at first sight between them, but over the course of the series they slowly develop a cautious relationship with each other.

The story plays out comically as a series of hijinks of misunderstandings and misidentifications as Ranma keeps accidentally switching between genders while trying to hide his curse from classmates. Behind all the

shrine maiden
A young female priestess who works as an attendant at a Shinto shrine, where she may clean and purify the shrine, offer prayers and blessings, and perform traditional ceremonies and rituals

Inuyasha

After she completed the *Ranma ½* manga, Rumiko Takahashi started a new but darker comedy adventure manga series in 1996 entitled *Inuyasha*. Drawing on Japanese mythology and folklore, *Inuyasha* follows a modern-day schoolgirl and shrine maiden named Kagome. When Kagome falls into a well, she is transported back to 1546, where she frees the half-demon Inuyasha from his imprisonment. It is revealed that Kagome is the reincarnation of her ancestor, Kikyo, who was Inuyasha's lover in the past. The story follows Kagome and Inuyasha as they bounce between the present and the past trying to gather the shards of the magical Shikon Jewel. In 2000 an anime series based on the manga debuted in Japan and was later broadcast in the United States on Cartoon Network. For many US fans, the *Inuyasha* anime was their first introduction to Takahashi's works, and it remains her best-known work in the United States.

laughs, the story presents a serious satire and critique of Japanese society. Traditionally, Japanese culture has had a fairly strict division between the genders and gender roles. Ranma's frequent transgressions as he switches between the genders highlights some of the arbitrariness and hypocrisy of Japanese attitudes. As a highly competitive martial artist, Ranma's self-image is tied up with being a strong male. Turning into a female, even one who is a powerful martial arts fighter, is an embarrassment for him. Over the course of the series, though, he learns to appreciate some of the roles he can play as a female that would not be acceptable as a male, such as enjoying sweet desserts. In anime and manga, it is typically women and girls who favor sweets.

Comic Misadventures

Akane, too, does not fit into traditional Japanese gender roles. She is a tomboy who prefers martial arts to the domestic arts and generally hates boys, which sets her apart from most of the other

Worldwide Popularity

While many manga-ka find popularity outside of Japan, Rumiko Takahashi is easily the most popular worldwide with both male and female fans. One writer attributes her popularity to humor that transcends borders and cultural differences. "The red thread that ties everything together is her humor, and that's what makes her work so popular both in Japan and overseas," says Lisandra Moor, a writer for a Tokyo-based English-language magazine. "Some have qualified her gags as 'international' as they often rely on imagery and context rather than dialogue and punch lines."

According to *Lambiek Comiclopedia*, Takahashi's works have been translated and published in nearly two dozen languages: Arabic, Chinese, Danish, Dutch, English, Finnish, French, German, Hebrew, Icelandic, Indonesian, Italian, Korean, Norwegian, Polish, Portuguese, Romanian, Russian, Spanish, Swedish, Turkish, and Vietnamese. Worldwide the number of printed books of her manga in 2024 exceeded 230 million.

Lisandra Moor, "How Rumiko Takahashi Contributed to the Popularity of Manga Overseas," *Tokyo Weekender*, February 15, 2019. www.tokyoweekender.com.

schoolgirls. She and Ranma are actually a good fit for each other, and part of the comedy is watching the lengths to which each goes to avoid admitting this fact to themselves and to each other. As anime scholar Susan J. Napier explains:

> This kind of complex plot, replete with humorous surprises involving gender transgression, is one that is familiar to Western audiences as well, at least as far back as the time of [Shakespeare's] *Twelfth Night*. Like the Shakespearian comedies and many others up until recently, the comic and fantastic nature of the plot, while thoroughly enjoyable on the surface, is also one that serves to hide or displace some important and serious issues of power and identity.[19]

As a manga, *Ranma ½* ran for 407 chapters. It ultimately introduces several dozen characters (including other victims of the cursed pools who must deal with their own transformations into various animals) and runs through a seemingly endless cycle of ever more ridiculous comic misadventures. Takahashi stretches out the story by never allowing Ranma and Akane to fully admit their feelings to one another. In an interview she explained why they never confessed their love to one another: "My feeling is that at the moment a manga's male and female leads say 'I love you,' it's like their story comes to an end. So because of that, it's important for them to not express that feeling in words. . . . I want my readers to be able to pick up, on their own, that two characters love each other. But I build it into my stories that the characters themselves don't quite realize it."[20]

The manga concludes on an unresolved note, with Ranma and Akane almost getting married, but their wedding is interrupted by all manner of chaos and delays. The final image is of the two of them running off together to school with the text implying that their story is not over yet.

Moving to Anime

Because of its huge success in Japan, *Ranma ½* was one of the first manga series licensed by Viz Media and brought to the United States in the early 1990s. After the text was translated into English, the artwork was flipped so that the progression of panels flowed from left to right as US comic books typically do. The first set of *Ranma ½* manga were published like US comics, as single twenty-two- to thirty-two-page issues that contained a single chapter. Soon after that, VIZ dropped the single-issue model and began publishing them in book form as the company continues to do today.

From 1989 through 1992, Studio Deen created 189 half-hour anime episodes of *Ranma ½* along with three theatrical films and

Rumiko Takahashi's* Ranma ½ *has reached American audiences both as a manga series and as a televised anime series (pictured). The latest reboot of the* Ranma ½ *anime series premiered worldwide on Netflix in 2024.

eleven direct-to-video releases. Even with all those adaptations, the studio only covered about 60 percent of the manga series' storyline and never reached the ending. VIZ Media licensed the anime series in 1993 to go along with its US release of the manga, so *Ranma ½* was one of the first anime series ever released on home video in the United States.

Recognition and Reboot

From the 1990s through the present, Takahashi's fame and popularity have spread throughout the world—and the professional comics establishment has taken notice. She has now won numerous awards and honors, including the Inkpot Award for cartoonists at the 1994 San Diego Comic-Con and inductions into the Will Eisner Comic Awards Hall of Fame in 2018 and the Harvey Awards (for comic artists) Hall of Fame in 2021. She was also made a knight of the Order of Arts and Letters by the French government in 2023.

In the fall of 2024, a reboot of the *Ranma ½* anime series premiered worldwide on Netflix. In November 2024 Netflix reported that the new *Ranma ½* ranked number six worldwide of all non-English shows on its platform, with over 1.4 million viewers. Takahashi's comic characters are now truly reaching a whole new generation of anime fans.

Naoko Takeuchi and *Sailor Moon*

Science and art have always been central to Naoko Takeuchi's world. The future creator of *Sailor Moon*, a major shōjo manga with astronomical elements, spent her high school years as a member of both the school's manga club and astronomy club. Takeuchi's interest in science led her to attend a college of pharmacy. Even while in college, she was already working on manga. She submitted a one-shot titled *Love Call* to the shōjo manga magazine *Nakayoshi*, where it was published in 1986 and won her the magazine's New Artist award. She followed up that early success with several more one-shot manga, and from 1989 to 1990 she partnered with a friend to create a short serial titled *Maria*. The next year she did another short series called *The Cherry Project* about a young girl named Cherry who is training to be a professional skater. In 1991 Takeuchi published another one-shot manga. This time the story was about a magical superhero girl named Sailor V. The story, titled *Codename: Sailor V*, was the genesis of her longer manga *Pretty Soldier Sailor Moon*. In this story Minako Aino (Sailor V) becomes Sailor Venus, one of the sidekicks of the main character, Sailor Moon.

Team Superheroes

Back in 1991 there were two major popular types of manga and anime series. The first was the "magical girl" genre, which told stories of ordinary girls who were given magical powers

sentai
"Squadron shows" in English; stories that follow groups of usually five costumed superheroes who band together to fight supernatural villains

and used them to perform good deeds. Usually, there was an animal sidekick, or magical familiar, and frequently characters had magical objects that enabled them to transform into their magical girl form. The second popular storyline was *sentai*, or squadron shows. These stories followed groups of usually five costumed superheroes who band together to fight supernatural villains. There were many dozens of these shows produced in Japan. One live-action version was even reworked and exported to the United States as *Mighty Morphin Power Rangers*. In this series, scenes of the characters in normal life were filmed with American actors, then the costumed fight scenes (with masks covering the actors' faces) were recycled from the original Japanese scenes. Takeuchi combined both of these ultra-popular elements to create her unique mash-up, *Sailor Moon*.

The *Sailor Moon* story begins with Usagi Tsukino, a fourteen-year-old girl in Tokyo who is not the ideal or perfect Japanese student. She is lazy, whiney, clumsy, and more interested in sleeping, eating, and playing video games than studying. She is approached

Naoko Takeuchi created a unique mash-up in her long-running Sailor Moon *series. She combines stories about ordinary girls who perform good deeds with the help of magical powers and stories about costumed superheroes who fight supernatural villains.*

by a talking cat named Luna who states that Usagi is actually the incarnation of the magical girl Sailor Moon. Luna gives her a brooch that causes her to transform whenever she shouts out "moon prism power, make up!" But even as a superhero, Usagi is still cowardly, clumsy, and completely incompetent when facing the supernatural villains she must fight. Initially, she almost loses her battles, until she is inspired at the last minute by the handsome young male superhero, Tuxedo Mask, and rallies to defeat the villain.

Over the course of her adventures, Usagi meets four more magical girls, or sailor guardians, each one named after a planet: Sailor Mercury, Sailor Mars, Sailor Jupiter, and Sailor Venus. The "sailor" portion of their names comes from the fact that all of their superhero costumes are based on Japanese schoolgirl uniforms, which resemble sailor suits. Joining together, the Guardians spend their nighttime hours fighting supernatural villains who threaten Tokyo—all while battling for justice, romance, and friendship. In keeping with her interest in natural science, Takeuchi named many of the villains after gems, minerals, and astronomical objects.

Inspired by Japanese and Greek Myths

The original manga ran for fifty-two chapters from 1991 through 1997 and covered five story arcs. In later story arcs, more charac-

Sailor Moon Stage Shows

In the United States, Disney often produces shows with live actors performing as characters from its animated films. The shows usually feature scenes from the movies along with song and dance numbers. These shows tour major cities around the country so fans can see an in-person version of the movie. In Japan stage shows of live actors re-creating scenes and songs from the *Sailor Moon* anime have also been popular. Performances began in Tokyo in 1993 soon after the anime debuted and have continued with new variations in the show and new actors every year since. Some of these shows have traveled overseas. Performances have taken place in Shanghai, China, New York, and Washington, DC. In the spring of 2025, a production of *Pretty Guardian Sailor Moon: The Super Live* made a tour of eighteen US cities, becoming the first large-scale tour of the franchise outside of Japan.

ters are introduced, including Sailor Saturn, Sailor Uranus, Sailor Neptune, Sailor Pluto, and a little girl known as Sailor Chibi Moon. Sailor Chibi Moon is Usagi's future daughter from her reincarnation in the thirtieth century and has been sent back to the present time. Ultimately, Usagi discovers her full backstory. She is the reincarnation of the original Princess Serenity of the Moon while the other four guardians were her protectors and Mamoru is the reincarnation of her forbidden lover, Prince Endymion of Earth. When the moon kingdom came under attack, her mother, Queen Serenity, sent them all to be reborn on Earth for their safety.

Takeuchi's Sailor Moon stories were inspired by both Greek and Japanese mythology. Prince Endymion is based on a character in Greek mythology who was the human lover of the moon goddess Selene. Various accounts say Endymion was either a shepherd or an astronomer, who spent most of his evenings gazing at the moon. Selene saw him from above and fell in love with his beauty. Usagi's backstory as a moon princess comes directly from an ancient and famous Japanese folktale, *The Tale of the Bamboo Cutter*. This story tells of a poor bamboo cutter and his wife who find and rear a magical baby girl who turns out to be the reincarnation of the moon princess. At the end of the story she regains her memories and must return to the moon.

Anime Success

Because of the manga's popularity, Tōei Animation (with financial backing by Bandai) produced an anime series that ran from 1992 to 1997. The series followed the five story arcs of the manga, with a different title each season to distinguish its arc: *Sailor Moon*, *Sailor Moon R*, *Sailor Moon S*, *Sailor Moon SuperS*, and *Sailor Moon Sailor Stars*. As the anime attracted growing audiences in Japan, *Sailor Moon* was exported for US television broadcast in 1995. It did not do well for the first two years, until Cartoon Network began rerunning it. Initially, only the first four seasons were broadcast in the United States, but the entire series was later released on home video.

The popularity of the Sailor Moon *manga series led to an anime series that followed five of the manga story arcs. One of these story arcs resulted in the film,* Sailor Moon R the Movie: The Promise of the Rose Year *(pictured).*

Favorable response to the anime on American TV prompted the publication of the translated manga as well. The publication of the *Sailor Moon* manga transformed the manga and comics publication industry in the United States. Up until this point, the vast majority of translated manga in the United States were shōnen manga: action-filled stories aimed at boys. Publishers assumed that girls would have no interest in manga, so they did not pursue stories that would appeal to girls. *Sailor Moon* proved them wrong. Once publishers realized they had a new, untapped market for manga, they rushed to put out more shōjo stories. Today US-published manga is split roughly evenly between shōnen and shōjo titles.

shōnen manga
Action-filled stories aimed at boys

When the Bandai corporation provided financial backing for *Sailor Moon*, it did so for the same reasons it backed *Gundam*: to sell lots of merchandise tied in with the series. With *Gundam*, the primary audience was males, and they wanted models of the robots to play with. For *Sailor Moon*, the primary audience was females, so other products had to be imagined and developed. It turned out that with its large number of primary characters, Bandai was able to create a wide variety of *Sailor Moon*–themed items. They did not just make action figures and dolls out of the main characters, they also designed and sold plush animals of the cats and an ever-increasing number of magical objects, wands, makeup, accessories, and transformational jewelry associated with each Sailor. These toys and objects allowed the fans to stretch their imaginations as they used the items to role-play and cosplay their favorite *Sailor Moon* characters.

Cultural Impact

While most anime are created just for entertainment, *Sailor Moon* has had a much wider cultural impact on its viewers in Japan, especially young girls. While women have more freedom than they used to in modern industrial societies like the United States and Japan, there are still long-standing cultural norms that girls are supposed to be wives or caregivers and not heroes. As anime scholar Anne Allison notes, the *Sailor Moon*

Gender Roles and Identity in *Sailor Moon*

In the first arc of the *Sailor Moon* manga and anime in Japan, two of the villains, Zoisite and Kunzite, were male and shown in a romantic relationship. When the anime was dubbed for North American broadcast in 1995, the producers changed Zoisite into a female character (he had long hair and effeminate facial features) to avoid presenting a gay couple on US television. Later in the series, the third arc introduces Haruka Tenoh and Michiru Kaioh (Sailor Uranus and Sailor Neptune). Both are older teenaged females, although Haruka races cars and dresses in masculine clothes. It is obvious from the storyline that the two are in a romantic relationship. Because there was no way to change Haruka's gender (particularly when she transforms into Sailor Uranus in a dress), the US production team rewrote the story. They described the pair as close cousins but left all the romantic imagery around them unchanged. US fans who knew the true story from the Japanese version protested, and this became one of the show's open secrets during its initial broadcast period in the 1990s.

stories are powerfully transformative because they show that "a 'normal' girl can . . . become a 'champion of justice' [and that] makes for a more balanced portrayal of heroism than the standard male scenario, in which the hero [is] focused and flawless from the beginning."[21]

The example of Usagi and the Sailor Guardians—where the anime female characters play leading roles in the action and conflict—provided Japanese girls with an effective, new type of role model. For instance, the female characters can now take the lead in determining their own lives and futures. In scholar Susan J. Napier's view, "Popular youth-oriented anime series such as . . . the 1990s *Sailor Moon* show images of powerful young women . . . that anticipate genuine, though small, changes in women's empowerment . . . and suggest alternatives to the notion of Japanese women as passive and domesticated."[22]

SOURCE NOTES

Introduction: The Making of Classic Anime and Manga

1. Casey Baseel, "Life-Size Gundam Statue to Appear in Osaka for the First Time Ever," Sora News 24, June 27, 2024. https://soranews24.com.
2. Casey Baseel, "*Ranma ½* Cafe Opening in Three Japanese Cities, Features Food with Transformable Flavors," Sora News 24, November 30, 2024. https://soranews24.com.

Chapter One: Kenji Miyazawa and *Night on the Galactic Railroad*

3. Quoted in Benjamin Ettinger, "Anime, Its Animators and the Art of Animation," Anipages, January 2, 2004. https://web.archive.org.
4. Justin Sevakis, "*Night on the Galactic Railroad*," Anime News Network, December 21, 2006. www.animenewsnetwork.com.

Chapter Two: Osamu Tezuka and *Astro Boy*

5. Helen McCarthy, *The Art of Osamu Tezuka: God of Manga*. New York: Abrams, 2009, p. 24.
6. McCarthy, *The Art of Osamu Tezuka*, p. 85.
7. McCarthy, *The Art of Osamu Tezuka*, p. 123.
8. Jonathan Clements, *Anime: A History*, 2nd ed. London: Bloomsbury, 2023, p. 177.
9. Quoted in McCarthy, *The Art of Osamu Tezuka*, p. 220.

Chapter Three: Hayao Miyazaki and *Nausicaä of the Valley of the Wind*

10. Quoted in Beth Cary and Frederik L. Schodt, trans., *Starting Point: 1979–1996*. San Francisco: VIZ Media, 2009, p. 70.
11. Quoted in Ryo Saitani, "I Understand Nausicaä a Bit More than I Did a Little While Ago," *Comic Box*, January 1995.
12. Quoted in Saitani, "I Understand Nausicaä a Bit More than I Did a Little While Ago."
13. Alicia Haddick, "Only Yesterday: Six Years After His Passing, Famed Studio Ghibli Animator Isao Takahata Is Honored in a Sweeping Retrospective," *Cinemascope*, April 11, 2024. https://letterboxd.com.

Chapter Four: Yoshiyuki Tomino and *Mobile Suit Gundam*

14. Quoted in Andrew Osmond, "Yoshiyuki Tomino: The Interview," *All the Anime* (blog), November 19, 2015. https://blog.alltheanime.com.

15. Quoted in NHK World Japan *Direct Talk*, *Anime Is Not to Be Underestimated: Yoshiyuki Tomino/Animation Director*, YouTube, 2022. www.youtube.com/watch?v=HS8Pyuij9M8.

Chapter Five: Riyoko Ikeda and *The Rose of Versailles*

16. Nobuko Anan, "*The Rose of Versailles*: Women and Revolution in Girls' Manga and the Socialist Movement in Japan," *Journal of Popular Culture*, March 29, 2014, p. 51.
17. Jonathan Clements and Helen McCarthy, *The Anime Encyclopedia*, 3rd rev. ed. Berkeley, CA: Stone Bridge, 2015, p. 702.
18. Quoted in Danica Davidson, "Making History: *The Rose of Versailles*," Anime News Network, October 30, 2012. www.animenewsnetwork.com.

Chapter Six: Rumiko Takahashi and *Ranma ½*

19. Susan J. Napier, *Anime from "Akira" to "Howl's Moving Castle": Experiencing Contemporary Japanese Animation*. New York: Palgrave Macmillan, 2005, p. 53.
20. Quoted in Casey Beseel, "Rumiko Takahashi Explains Why Her Characters Can't Ever Just Come Right Out and Say 'I Love You,'" Sora News 24, June 11, 2021. https://soranews24.com.

Chapter Seven: Naoko Takeuchi and *Sailor Moon*

21. Anne Allison, *Millennial Monsters: Japanese Toys and the Global Imagination*. Berkeley: University of California Press, 2006. Kindle edition.
22. Napier, *Anime from "Akira" to "Howl's Moving Castle,"* p. 33.

FOR FURTHER RESEARCH

Books

Jonathan Clements, *Anime: A History*. 2nd ed. London: Bloomsbury, 2023.

Jonathan Clements and Helen McCarthy, *The Anime Encyclopedia: A Century of Japanese Animation*. 3rd rev. ed. Berkeley, CA: Stone Bridge, 2015.

Insight Editions, *A History of Modern Manga (1952–2022)*. San Rafael, CA: Insight Editions, 2023.

Helen McCarthy, *The Art of Osamu Tezuka: God of Manga*. New York: Abrams, 2009.

Kenji Miyazawa, *"Night on the Galactic Railroad" and Other Stories from Ihatov*. Trans. Julianne Neville. Long Island City, NY: One Peace, 2020.

Susan Napier, *Miyazakiworld: A Life in Art*. New Haven, CT: Yale University Press, 2018.

Deborah Scally, *Miyazaki and the Hero's Journey*. Jefferson, NC: McFarland, 2022.

Frederik L. Schodt, *The Astro Boy Essays: Osamu Tezuka, Mighty Atom, and the Manga/Anime Revolution*. Berkeley, CA: Stone Bridge, 2007.

Frederik L. Schodt, *Manga! Manga! The World of Japanese Comics*. Rev. ed. New York: Kodansha, 2013.

Internet Sources

Sam Barsanti, "A Beginner's Guide to 40 Years of Robots, Rivals, and Sci-Fi Pacifism from *Mobile Suit Gundam*," AV Club, April 7, 2019. www.avclub.com.

Kyle DeGuzman, "What Is Anime—Origins, Evolution and Modern Examples," Studiobinder, January 14, 2025. www.studiobinder.com.

James Saunders-Wyndham, "The History of Japanese Manga: Ancient Art to Pop Culture," Romancing Japan, 2023. www.romancing-japan.com.

Websites

Ghibli Wiki
www.nausicaa.net/wiki/Main_Page
This is a fan-run English-language website that contains an encyclopedia of information about Hayao Miyazaki, his works, Studio Ghibli, and many of the other anime connected to them.

Gundam Wiki
https://gundam.fandom.com/wiki/The_Gundam_Wiki
This is a fan-run and publicly editable wiki about the Gundam universe. It lists all the series, plots, characters, mecha, and community discussions about all the series.

Rose of Versailles Wiki
https://rose-of-versailles.fandom.com/wiki/Rose_of_Versailles_Wiki
This is a fan-run, English-language wiki covering the manga and anime of *The Rose of Versailles*. It lists all the characters and outlines the stories in the manga and anime.

Rumic World
www.furinkan.com/index.html
This is a fan-run, English-language wiki about Rumiko Takahashi. It has information about all of her manga series and the anime series based on her manga, along with interviews of Takahashi and other articles about her work.

Sailor Moon Wiki
https://sailormoon.fandom.com/wiki/Sailor_Moon_Wiki
This is a fan-run wiki about *Sailor Moon*. It covers the manga, anime series, video games, live-action stage shows, and characters. It also has links to the *Sailor Moon* wikis in nine other languages.

Tezuka Osamu Official
https://tezukaosamu.net/en
This is the English-language version of the official Osamu Tezuka website maintained by Tezuka Productions. It gives the history of Tezuka's career, illustrated lists of all his major manga and anime series, and a list of Tezuka's messages and themes in his work.

World of Kenji Miyazawa
www.kenji-world.net/english
This is the English-language version of a Japanese website about Kenji Miyazawa. It includes sections about Miyazawa's life, information on his writings and characters, several essays about his work, and a listing of publications of his books and stories translated into English.

INDEX